MAKING THE PLAY

VOLLEYBALL

BY VALERIE BODDEN

CREATIVE EDUCATION • CREATIVE PAPERBACKS

Published by Creative Education and Creative Paperbacks
P.O. Box 227, Mankato, Minnesota 56002
Creative Education and Creative Paperbacks
are imprints of The Creative Company
www.thecreativecompany.us

Design and production by The Design Lab
Art direction by Rita Marshall
Printed in the United States of America

Photographs by iStockphoto (skynesher, t_kimura), Shutterstock (bahri altay, DnDavis, donatas1205, dotshock, Golbay, Jayakumar, muzsy, ostill, Solis Images, StefanoT, stockphotograf, supergenijalac, Dan Thornberg), Thinkstock (omgimages)

Library of Congress Cataloging-in-Publication Data
Bodden, Valerie.
Volleyball / Valerie Bodden.
p. cm. — (Making the play)
Includes index.
Summary: An elementary introduction to the physics involved in the sport of volleyball, including scientific concepts such as gravity and acceleration, and actions such as bumping and spiking.
ISBN 978-1-60818-658-7 (hardcover)
ISBN 978-1-62832-237-8 (pbk)
ISBN 978-1-56660-689-9 (eBook)
1. Volleyball—Juvenile literature. 2. Physics—Juvenile literature. I. Title.

GV1015.3.B64 2016
796.325—dc23   2015007573

CCSS: RI.1.1, 2, 3, 4, 5, 6, 7; RI.2.1, 2, 3, 5, 6, 7, 10; RI.3.1, 3, 5, 7, 8; RF.2.3, 4; RF.3.3

First Edition HC 9 8 7 6 5 4 3 2 1
First Edition PBK 9 8 7 6 5 4 3 2 1

AUG – 1 2016

CONTENTS

VOLLEYBALL AND SCIENCE

The volleyball soars through the air. You jump to spike it over the net. It smacks to the ground on the other side. Point!

POINT!

Do you think about science when you play volleyball? Probably not. But you use science anyway. A science called physics *(FIZ-icks)* can help you hit the ball and score. Let's see how!

FORCE AND GRAVITY

A force is any push or pull. You apply a force to something. It applies an equal force on you. The two forces push against each other.

Think of a swimmer pushing off a pool wall. The swimmer pushes on the wall. But the wall pushes on the swimmer, too. This sends the swimmer away.

You bump a volleyball up. The ball

pushes down on you at the same time.

The ball will go up for a while. Then

gravity will pull it back down.

GRAVITY

A force that pulls all objects toward the earth

13

ACCELERATION

When an object **accelerates** (*ak-SEL-uh-rates*), it changes speed or direction. Think of a car. The car slows down for a stop sign. It gets faster to move again.

An object with a smaller **mass** accelerates more. A volleyball has a smaller mass than you do. When you hit the ball, it changes speed and direction.

Your body accelerates, too. You change speed or direction to run across the court. Can you use acceleration when you serve? Give it a try, and make the play!

ACCELERATION ON THE MOVE

Mass affects which object will accelerate more when two objects crash.

WHAT YOU NEED

- A ramp
- Ping-Pong ball
- Golf ball

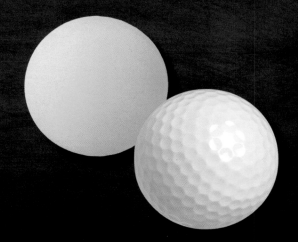

WHAT YOU DO

Put the golf ball at the bottom of the ramp. Roll the Ping-Pong ball down the ramp so that it crashes into the golf ball. How far does the golf ball move? Now switch the balls and try it again. How far do the balls move this time? Next, roll both down the ramp at the same time. Which one goes faster? Which goes farther? What does this tell you about mass and acceleration?

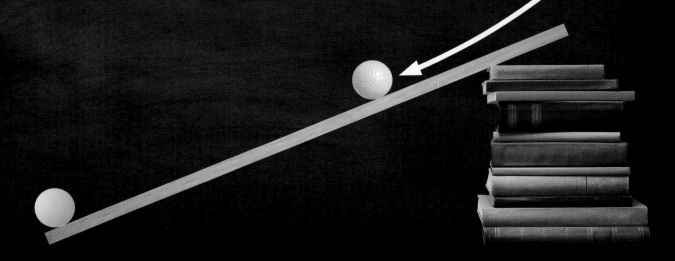

GLOSSARY

accelerates-changes speed or direction, usually getting faster

mass-the amount of material that makes up an object

READ MORE

Gifford, Clive. *Basketball and Other Ball Sports*. Mankato, Minn.: Amicus, 2012.

Gore, Bryson. *Physics*. Mankato, Minn.: Stargazer, 2009.

Walton, Ruth. *Let's Go to the Playground*. Mankato, Minn.: Sea-to-Sea, 2013.

WEBSITES

Idaho Public Television: Force and Motion
http://idahoptv.org/ dialogue4kids/season12/force _and_motion/facts.cfm
Learn more about the forces that are all around you.

StudyJams! Newton's Third Law: Action & Reaction
http://studyjams.scholastic.com /studyjams/jams/science/forces -and-motion/action-and -reaction.htm
Check out this video about how forces and acceleration work.

NOTE: Every effort has been made to ensure that the websites listed above are suitable for children, that they have educational value, and that they contain no inappropriate material. However, because of the nature of the Internet, it is impossible to guarantee that these sites will remain active indefinitely or that their contents will not be altered.

INDEX